VisionCrafting

A Self-Guided Journey

Lynn Hayes

Go confidently in the
direction of your dreams.
Live the life you have imagined.

--Henry David Thoreau

All material herein is copyright © by Lynn Hayes, 2009.

All rights to this material are reserved. No part of this book may be reproduced for public use, other than for "fair use" as brief quotations in articles or reviews, without prior permission of the author.

Cover design: Joanna Powell Colbert, www.gaiandesign.com.

Disclaimer: The author of this book does not dispense medical advice, nor is this book intended as a prescription for the treatment of medical or emotional illness without the advice of a physician. Rather, this book is intended as an aid for your quest for spiritual and emotional well-being, and the author takes no responsibility for any negative outcome that arises as the result of its use.

ISBN 978-1448685929

First printing September 2009

Printed in the United States of America

Grateful acknowledgement is made for the use of mandalas by Paul Heussenstam, whose work can be viewed on the web at www.mandalas.com, and to Joanna Powell Colbert, whose beautiful artwork graces the cover of this book. Thanks also go to Maxine Mills whose expert guidance shaped the layout of this book.

I have purchased the rights for other images that appear throughout this book, but a few of these images were found on the internet without attribution and I apologize in advance for any unforeseen copyright violation

I am deeply indebted for the inspiration of many dear friends and an ex-husband or two without whom I would have never began this journey of self-improvement.

I also give thanks for the inspiration of those who came before me including, but not limited to, Dr. Wayne Dyer, Deepak Chopra, and Anthony Robbins.

I am particularly grateful to my husband Rich, whose endless patience and encouragement has helped me to blossom and continue to grow into my potential. And last but not least, I thank the stars and planets that have taught and inspired me from childhood to reach beyond the boundaries of ordinary limitations, and the thousands of clients I have worked with over the years who have been the greatest teachers of all.

"The future belongs to those who believe in the beauty of their dreams."

--Eleanor Roosevelt

Our dreams are messages from the Spirit within us, calling us forth to our destiny. We have only to listen to these messages and allow our dreams to take flight. They will guide us along the path to their fulfillment, and deconstruct all of the blocks that keep us from realizing our true potential.

Table of Contents

Preface --- 4
How to use this book -- 13
Chapter One: My own story ------------------------------------- 15
Chapter Two: History of the Law of Attraction --------------- 19
Chapter Three: Modern Physics and the Nature of Reality - 25
Chapter Four: What are beliefs? ------------------------------- 31
Chapter Five: Visioncrafting in a financial crisis ------------- 36
Chapter Six: What is a life of abundance? -------------------- 38
Chapter Seven: What abundance is NOT -------------------- 42
Chapter Eight: Principles of abundance ---------------------- 45
1. We create our own reality ---------------------------------- 45
2. That which we focus on expands -------------------------- 49
3. Abundance is available in infinite supply ----------------- 51
4. Giving and receiving occur in balance -------------------- 51
5. Gratitude expands our ability to receive ----------------- 54
6. Holding on is the result of a belief in shortage ----------- 57
7. Each moment offers the freedom for conscious choice -- 60
8. Conscious creation requires a balance -------------------- 63
Chapter Nine: The crafting of wishes ------------------------- 67
Chapter Ten: Obstacles that keep us from our dreams ----- 79
Chapter Eleven: Creating a new vision ----------------------- 84
Chapter Twelve: Examples to help you get started --------- 93
Chapter Thirteen: Now it's your turn! ------------------------- 103
Chapter Fourteen: Developing a Practice -------------------- 107
Chapter Fifteen: Visioncrafting for a lifetime ---------------- 110

Preface

As an astrologer, I study the cycles of time and their effect on human behavior. During the period in which Pluto traveled through Sagittarius (from 1995 until 2008), our world saw an unprecedented expansion of wealth and prosperity. Sagittarius is the sign of faith, optimism and beliefs, and Pluto is the planet that brings transformation and change as well as compulsive behavior.

Under the influence of Pluto in Sagittarius, the self-help industry exploded into a plethora of books on prosperity, abundance, and strategies for life change. But these ideas are nothing new. The Universal Law of Attraction, made so famous by 2008's well-marketed book and DVD called **The Secret**, has been around for many years.

So why have I written yet another book to help people to improve their lives?

Over the years I have consulted with a few thousand astrology clients, most of whom sought my services because they needed change in their lives. The astrology reading clarified the underlying issues behind their experiences, thoughts and behavior and this was useful, but without new tools to make lasting changes they were still stuck in old patterns and beliefs.

Positive thinking and affirmations can go only so far – to create real change in our lives we must discover the core beliefs that underlie everything that we do and feel. I have studied what I call "performance technology" over the past twenty years and have combined the best features and techniques from many different modalities to create what I call the Visioncrafting process. This is not just another visualization program – this process helps you to uncover the core beliefs that underpin your own reality. Then we can transform those beliefs in order to create a more effective and joyful experience throughout our lives.

This is not an astrology book, but because I am an astrologer I look at life through the lens of the astrological symbolism. Studying the movement of the planets and their cycles helps to provide a framework within which we can most effectively create change in our life. The cycles of Pluto are particularly significant in any kind of transformative work. Prosperity and abundance work was easy when Pluto was in Sagittarius between 1995 and 2008. Pluto's travels through Sagittarius brought an overabundance of faith and optimism and an experience of life's limitless potential was easy to achieve.

The expansiveness of the Pluto in Sagittarius era is now behind us and in 2008 we entered the contraction of Pluto in Capricorn. Capricorn is the sign that challenges us to let go of our fantasies and face the cold hard reality of life. Under the Capricorn influence blind belief is no longer enough – we must have practical applications and strategies to make real change in the fundamentals of our belief systems.

Visioncrafting combines a detailed and practical system with the magic of the power of intention. This process has worked for me in my life, and I have seen it change the lives of many of my clients in ways that are thrilling and beautiful. I offer it to you with the greatest love and respect for the beauty of the soul that you are, and with blessings for the positive outcome that you desire.

As you begin this journey, you must leave your old rules behind. You'll learn how to recognize belief systems that hold you back, and how to let go of patterns of thinking that keep you stuck in a life that offers less than the life you have dreamed of. You'll learn practical tools to retrain the subconscious mind so that it will support you as you open your heart and soul to the magic of creation.

Visioncrafting is magic, but it requires a certain amount of commitment and focus. Go at your own pace and don't rush the process. If you stick with me all the way to the end of the book, the doorway will begin to open and your new visions will begin to take hold.

How to use this book

This book was adapted from the workbooks I use in my live Visioncrafting workshops, so it follows the same format with each section building on the section before it. Nearly every section asks questions designed to get you thinking and evaluating your life from a new perspective.

Chances are you were drawn to this book because you have a desire to create change in your life. Because our outer world mirrors our internal beliefs and desires, an internal shift needs to occur before the outer reflection of our life can integrate the change.

As you will find, creating lasting change and transformation requires more than positive thinking and setting an intention. We need to delve into the subconscious mind where our most powerful belief systems lie, and we can, using the tools in this workbook, discover what is holding us back and keeping us from realizing our dreams.

I suggest that you not rush through the process, but take your time as you read through this book. Some of this material may be familiar to you, but by making the choice to read this book, and in sitting down to begin the Visioncrafting program, you have set an intention to create change in your life. This will open doorways in the conscious and subconscious mind that will help you to assimilate it in a completely new way.

I highly recommend that you utilize all of the space I've provided for you to take notes throughout the book, and you may also want to begin keeping a journal as the transformation begins to unfold. The change that you experience may seem very small at first, and paying attention to each small step can help to inspire us to continue.

Please follow every step as outlined in each chapter, and take as much time as you need. At the end of the workbook I've outlined the steps you will want to take to make this a successful ongoing practice which will help you to consistently reinforce the changes that are happening within you.

Don't be surprised if you encounter a bit of fear and inner resistance along the way as the belief systems that you have depended on to create security lose their power and begin to fall away. If you feel any anxiety or disturbance, simply take a break. Turn your attention within and discover the nature of these fears or anxieties from subconscious. Make notes of these areas of discomfort in your journal, and then incorporate these fears later when you begin to work with your new vision. Identifying the fears that have held you back in the past is a valuable part of this process, and it will help you to achieve real transformation at core levels.

Consistency is the key to any kind of successful practice, and that is just as true with Visioncrafting. If you read the book once and do the exercises and then put it away, you will experience some benefit. But if you consistently apply the principles in your own life, you will experience magic!

If you find you need coaching to help you to stay on track or to define your goals, I am available to help. Visit my website for more information on personal coaching and consultations:

www.astrodynamics.net.

Chapter One:
My own story and the birth of the Visioncrafting process

In 1980, I lived in a trailer home, had no relationship with my family, and struggled from one failed relationship to another including a brand new divorce from a man I had never even liked. I had barely enough money to pay my $150/month rent and my car had died. This was the most difficult time of my life, but it was also the beginning of my awakening.

I share my story with you here in these pages because I am living proof that the Visioncrafting process works. There is nothing exceptional about me, and the process can work for you too. It takes only determination and the willingness to make a change in your life.

I had spent the early part of my life in a family in which the primary means of communication was through rage and emotional violence, and I was the victim of a sexual assault at the age of ten. I had explored nearly every available drug beginning in my teens, and at the age of 20 I began a lifelong practice of meditation which very likely saved my life.

Along the way I became fascinated with astrology, and after I hit that bottom point in 1980 I met the astrologer Steven Forrest who lived here in Chapel Hill at the time. Steven started me in my training, teaching me to cast charts and how to synthesize them. Soon I was doing charts for friends and friends of friends, and learning more about the complex dynamics that made up my own difficult chart.

Eventually in 1985 I married a good and kind man who gave me my first lesson in creating my own reality. Working from a pamphlet entitled *"The Lazy Man's Guide to Riches,"* we worked together to expand our rental real estate business. I had just begun my own career as a real estate agent (in those days it was the very rare astrologer who could make a living), and the idea of setting goals to accomplish financial objectives took hold. We were pretty impressed with the degree of financial success and real estate acquisitions that we achieved as a result of the financial goals we set.

Unfortunately, I was still not emotionally capable of sustaining a committed relationship and the marriage ended in 1990. The years between 1990 and 1995 were both the worst and the best of my life up to that point. My pain over the loss of my marriage motivated me to delve into deep soul searching. My first step was the Tony Robbins Personal Power program, which I followed religiously for the prescribed 30 days. The Personal Power program goes beyond goals and affirmations and asks probing questions to help one identify destructive behavior patterns. I learned that I really knew very little about myself and what I actually wanted out of life. The program inspired me to establish goals and create a vision for how I wanted the rest of my life to be, not just financially but in every area of my life.

Itt wasn't until after my divorce in 1990 that I began to study psychological astrology. The failure of my marriage drove me to learn all I could about the dynamics of human relationships and the psychological dynamics behind them. My study of Jungian psychology deepened my practice even more, helping me to assist clients in better integrating the psychological dynamics as shown in the birth chart.

During this time I also began experimenting with various modalities of magic and learning more about ways that we can focus our conscious intention in order to create our reality. Over time I developed the process of using language as a tool of transformation and to develop a vision that forms the basis of a new empowerment and a new life. Because this is such a dynamic process, when I incorporated these tools into my astrological practice I decided to call my practice Astrodynamics.

The birthchart reading helps to identify the psychological issues and complexes that create frustration, but it also reveals the gifts and tools that can help us to unlock the doors which keep us from living a creative and happy life. But once we recognize the source of our blocks and difficulties, we need to go a step or two further so that we can integrate and transform these challenges into gifts that fully empower and assist us to live a life that is full of love and wonder.

The process that I call "Visioncrafting" helps us to reframe and repattern old belief systems and dysfunctional behavior patterns so that we become newly liberated and able to achieve virtually anything that we wish for.

My life has been transformed in the most incredible ways since I began this journey. My personality has evolved from a frightened, negative and sulky girl to a confident, empowered and loving woman. I attracted and recognized a soul mate relationship and have been happily married since 1999. We built the home that I had first imagined over 10 years before, on five acres with a pond, and I have financial assets beyond what I ever dreamed possible with three successful businesses including a worldwide astrology clientele.

But beyond this, I have achieved a level of personal satisfaction and peace that I never imagined was possible for me. I feel powerfully connected to the flow of the Universe and possess a deep and abiding trust and faith in the wisdom of the supreme Intelligence that guides us all. The comfort of this connection is the greatest abundance that I could have imagined.

In 2005 it became obvious to me that financial success and assets were not enough; I had a deep longing for a greater spiritual connection and a work schedule that would encourage a peace and serenity that was lacking at the time. I added this desire to my Vision list, and it didn't take long before my work life adjusted so that this desire could be accommodated. Now I have time to smell the roses and a work life that is balanced, harmonious and happy.

I have used the Visioncrafting process with hundreds of clients. I can't say that it has worked for everyone, but I CAN say that it has worked for everyone who has made the process a consistent practice. Some clients have become discouraged when they did not see immediate results, and occasionally a client is deeply invested in their pain and distress and unwilling to shift into a different mindset. Changing our life often means letting go of who we think we are, and that can be very difficult for some of us.

Some changes take more time than others. If we want to lose weight, we first need to uncover and work through the reasons why we gained weight in the first place. If we want to attract a partner, we must first face our fears of intimacy or a lack of self-confidence. But in holding a vision of these experiences that we desire, our bodies, our mind and our entire nervous system begins to participate in the changes that need to occur in order for our dreams to come true.

Now you can discover the magic of the Visioncrafting process on your own, with this self-guided workbook. Follow each step at your own pace; there are no rules or requirements and no final exams. I ask only that you make this process a consistent practice and watch as your life begins to unfold with beauty, magic and adventure.

Lynn Hayes
July 2009

Chapter Two:
History of the "Law of Attraction"

The idea that we create our own reality is nothing new. For thousands of years the law of karma in Hindu philosophy proposed that what we do in one life creates our reality in the next. Writers in the nineteenth century in the Transcendalist movement drew upon Hindu philosophy to devise new ways of thinking in the West.

One Transcendalist writer was Ralph Waldo Emerson. In 1870 Emerson wrote a book called **Success** in which he said, "We live among gods of our own creation." He went on to say,

> The fundamental fact in our metaphysic constitution is the correspondence of man to the world, so that every change in that writes a record in the mind. The mind yields sympathetically to the tendencies or law which stream through things and make the order of Nature; and in the perfection of this correspondence or expressiveness, the health and force of man consist.[1]

Around this same time, a philosophical movement known as *New Thought* was developing around ideas that the mind could be

---

[1] **Success**, by Ralph Waldo Emerson. Available in the public domain on several websites including www.infomotions.com.

used to heal the sick. Its original proponent appears to have been Phineas Parkhurst Quimby, who began studying Mesmerism (hypnosis) in 1838. Although he had no formal medical training he was called Doctor by his associates and patients. He was particularly interested in the placebo effect of the mind over the body that was recognized even in those days. Mary Baker Eddy, founder of the religion called Christian Science, was a patient of Dr. Quimby. His radical new ideas included this one:

> "The trouble is in the mind, for the body is only the house for the mind to dwell in . . . [I]f your mind has been deceived by some invisible enemy into a belief, you have put it into the form of a disease, with or without your knowledge. Disease ... unwittingly develops by impressing wrong thoughts and mental pictures upon the subconscious spiritual matter."[2]

The rise of the New Thought movement corresponds to the entry of Pluto into Gemini between 1882 and 1912. Pluto creates changes and transformation in the areas ruled by the sign through which it travels, and Gemini is the sign of ideas and communication. Under the Geminian influence new ideas are examined without an effort made to ascertain their truth, so a multitude of new thoughts and philosophies can be entertained without the need for judgment. Pluto deals with issues of power, and Gemini the mind and intellect so it is not surprising that the power of the mind became the prevailing philosophical consideration.

Coincidentally, Albert Einstein formulated his theory of relativity during this period as well, forever transforming our understanding of the nature of reality.

What we now call the Law of Attraction was a focus of the studies of the Theosophists, especially Annie Besant whose 1901 book **Thought Power** is available free in the public domain at the-secrets-of-the-law-of-attraction.com. Besant and other Theosophist writers were primarily concerned with the application of the powers of thought to the spiritual experience, rather than to the material world.

---

[2] Phineas Quimby, **The Complete Writings**, Ervin Seale, ed. Vol. 3; page 208. Devorss (1988).

James Allen, another New Thought writer, expounded in 1902 upon the power of thought to create a man's character and destiny: "The soul attracts that which it secretly harbors, that which it loves, and also that which it fears. It reaches the height of its cherished aspirations. It falls to the level of its unchastened desires - and circumstances are the means by which the soul receives its own." [3]

In 1906 William Walker Atkinson may have been the first writer to use the term Law of Attraction:

> We speak learnedly of the Law of Gravitation, but ignore that equally wonderful manifestation, THE LAW OF ATTRACTION IN THE THOUGHT WORLD. ...
>
> When we come to see that Thought is a force - a manifestation of energy - having a magnet-like power of attraction, we will begin to understand the why and wherefore of many things that have heretofore seemed dark to us. ...
>
> We have passed through the age of physical force on to the age of intellectual [relating astrologically to the sign of Gemini] supremacy [corresponding to the influence of Pluto], and are now entering a new and almost unknown field, that of psychic power.[4]

Shortly thereafter, in 1907 New Thought writer Bruce MacLelland wrote a book which advocated using the power of thought specifically for the purpose of creating prosperity and wealth, perhaps for the very first time:

---

[3] James Allen, **As a Man Thinketh – Effect of Thought on Circumstance.** Available in the public domain at www.jamesallenlibrary.com which is also a wonderful source of inspirational quotes from Mr. Allen.
[4] William Walker Atkinson, **Thought Vibration**, available in the public domain and online at www.psitek,.net.

The study of mental language and power of suggestion showed clearly that confidence concerning one's ability to do could be developed, and that the belief made the doing possible. ...

This subconscious mind is a magnet of attractive and repellent qualities. It receives thought, a literal element, and sends it out again reinforced in volume and intensity in proportion to the operating power of the will. It is attractive in its relation to the Supreme at all times and receives power from the Force of Nature. It is the operating force which gains health, fame and wealth.[5]

Much of the 2008 bestseller **The Secret** is based on a book by Wallace Wattles written in 1910 called **The Science of Getting Rich**. Wattles, a student of Emerson and Hegel, was one of the first proponents of Creative Visualization and his book is freely available on the internet since it is now in the public domain. [6]

Wattles' work was extremely significant for its time and contains many of the principles that we use today, such as the importance of gratitude: "Gratitude brings your whole mind into closer harmony with the creative energies of the universe." He also admonished that one's willpower should not be used on other people and that one should not seek power over others, principles which carry wisdom even today.

In the early 1920s Émile Coué, a French psychologist, introduced a concept called "optimistic autosuggestion" which was essentially the repetition of a positive statement in order to obtain a specific result. Coué's work was groundbreaking in that rather than focusing on the conscious will to achieve a goal, Coué felt that changing one's life required a change in the subconscious mind through the use of imagination. Coué's subjects utilized a ritual which involved repeating affirmations daily.

---

[5] Bruce MacClelland, **Prosperity Through Thought-Force**, available in the public domain and online at www.confidentlifestyle.com.
[6] http://en.wikisource.org/wiki/The_Science_of_Getting_Rich.

Coue's work was essentially autohypnosis that focused upon changing the conscious mind by exercising the subconscious. He wrote:

> If you persuade yourself that you can do a certain thing, provided this thing be possible, you will do it however difficult it may be. If on the contrary you imagine that you cannot do the simplest thing in the world, it is impossible for you to do it, and molehills become for you unscalable mountains.[7]

Shortly thereafter Ernest Holmes founded the Church of Religious Science in 1927, based on the Science of Mind precepts, including the concept of "Affirmative Prayer" in which one states the outcome of a prayer as if it has already happened. These concepts form the basis of affirmations as they are used today.

The following year, Napoleon Hill (author of the best-seller **Think and Grow Rich**[8] published in 1937) published a study course called the Law of Success based on what he called the Philosophy of Achievement.

Hill is widely considered to be the grandfather of the self-help movement, and his book became one of the best-selling works of all time, selling over 60 million copies.

Hill combined the pursuit of wealth and riches with an aspiration for increased spiritual growth and power, and outlined a thirteen-step path for accomplishing this goal. However, his techniques still relied on the focus on positive thinking and avoidance of negative emotions which as we have come to see is not sufficient to create lasting change.

In 1952 Norman Vincent Peale, a Protestant preacher, published his best-selling book **The Power of Positive Thinking**.

---

[7] Emile Coué, **Self-Mastery through Autosuggestion**, available in the public domain and online at http://www.psitek.net/pages/PsiTekSMTCAContents.html.

[8] Napoleon Hill, **Think and Grow Rich**, available in the public domain at www.sacred-texts.com/nth/tgr.

Again, the conscious mind, along with faith and prayer, was used to focus on positive outcomes in the hopes of bringing about the desired result

During the 1960s popular psychology was more about self-acceptance than transformation. Books such as **I'm OK, You're OK** lined the shelves of modern readers and there was less of a focus on life transformation until the late 1970s and early 1980s. At this time writers such as Louise Hay and Wayne Dyer began promoting the ideas of using positive thinking to effect healing and transformation in everyday lives, and the use of affirmations and positive thinking began to penetrate into the mainstream. This led to a widening field of motivational speakers and experts in success technology such as Jim Rohn, Zig Zieglar, Brian Tracy and others.

Wayne Dyer's work focuses on what he calls the Law of Intention rather than the Law of Attraction. "You don't attract what you want, you attract what you *are* [emphasis added].[9] Dyer's books such as **Manifest your Destiny** combined spiritual wisdom with a discussion of the power of intention to create a better life. Dyer was one of the first modern writers to bridge the spiritual realm with the realm of success and achievement, breaking new ground.

The research and success strategies developed by Anthony Robbins lifted the new field of motivation and performance enhancement to new heights with his detailed 30-day program to effect change and personal transformation. For the first time, masses of people learned concrete steps to design a more effective life for themselves.

These philosophies and in some cases religions (Science of Mind, Christian Science) are uniquely American in origin. We could argue that the American focus on self-mastery and the "self-made man" (and woman) is a powerful part of the American dream.

Regardless of how these philosophies originated, it is clear that they not only remain with us but that they have been honed and polished over the last 100 years. And now, in the twenty-first

---

[9] Article by Valerie Grieber, *The Power of Intention*, from www.drwaynedyer.com.

century, the pathways of the Law of Attraction, positive thinking, quantum physics, spiritual principles, and the power of intention have converged in a magical awareness of the interconnectedness of the soul, the mind, and the world to create reality.

Next we'll explore the ways in which modern science have opened doorways to understanding this magic even further.

Chapter Three:
Modern physics and the nature of reality

Beginning with Albert Einstein back in the early 1900s, modern physics has been turning our understanding of the nature of reality upside down. Each new discovery forever transforms our knowledge of the workings of the Universe.

Before quantum theory, the human understanding of matter had not changed since Isaac Newton's universal laws of motion of the 18th century. It is ironic that Newton's laws were used by scientists over the next 200 years to establish the primacy of the material world, because Newton himself was an alchemist and an occultist, and a student of the ancient mystery schools of wisdom.

After Newton, science became a process of "reductionism," where pieces of reality are taken apart and studied so that their behavior can be reliably predicted. This in fact became known as the scientific method. However, scientists in the early 20th century formulated new theories that the Universe consists of an entanglement of energy waves rather than a solid mass of matter.

Under this "entanglement" theory, two objects behave synchronously with no intermediary and can somehow sense and affect each other from a distance, with no direct contact. Albert Einstein called this idea "spooky," and was never able to reconcile it with his idea of relativity which was a much more grounded approach to the nature of reality: a fixed relationship between matter and energy. Einstein wanted to believe that "God does not play dice" and believed that no communication can travel faster than the speed of light.

Recent scientific discoveries and theories are turning our understanding of the nature of objective reality inside out. Some scientists have proposed a "holographic theory of the Universe," in which reality is merely a projection of our consciousness onto our brains. In this theory, which mirrors to a great extent the wisdom of the ancient Vedic scriptures which taught that reality is an illusion and only consciousness is real, it is consciousness that influences the brain and not the other way around.

According to British physicist Sir James Jeans:

"The stream of human knowledge is impartially heading towards a non-mechanical reality. The universe begins to look more like a great thought than a great machine. Mind no longer appears to be an accidental intruder into the realm of matter. We are beginning to suspect that we ought rather to hail it as the creator and governor of this realm."

Physics is not the only field undergoing a paradigm shift. Biologists have discovered that unlike the conventional idea that our genes control our mind and our health, our consciousness and perception of our environment actually turn certain genes on and off without affecting the DNA. If stress can turn genes on and off, argue scientists like Dr. Bruce Lipton, author of **The Biology of Belief**[10], then so can the thoughts of the conscious and subconscious mind.

---

[10] Bruce Lipton, **Biology of Belief**, Mountain of Love Publishing 2005.

Getting back to the physical nature of reality, a new theory called "biocentrism" attempts to tie together all of the loose ends of Einstein's theories and quantum physics by proposing that consciousness creates the Universe, rather than the other way around. In biocentrism, space and time are matters of perception and without the presence of consciousness matter exists solely in a state of probability. It is consciousness that sets matter in motion. Dr. Robert Lanza[11] is one of the fathers of this new conceptualization of our Universe as a living, breathing being in which all facets of life are interwoven and that consciousness is the factor that creates change.

The introduction of the concept of consciousness, which for thousands of years was considered solely the province of religion, into a discussion of the workings of the Universe is a huge paradigm shift for scientists. It appears to solve the "Theory of Everything" that has been the Holy Grail of physicists for nearly a century, and it correlates nicely to beliefs found in the world's ancient wisdom traditions.

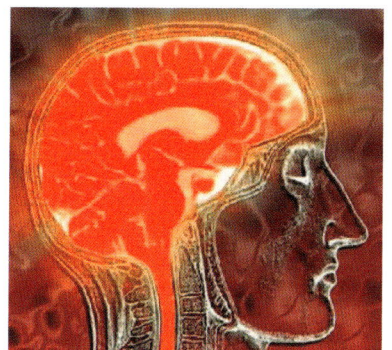

Scientists are just starting to get on board with the idea that our mind creates our reality, but for hundreds of years the placebo effect has proven the power of the mind to create healing and to create disease.

A recent study[12] found that brain scans in fourteen young, healthy men demonstrated that when they were told they were to receive a medicine to relieve their pain, endorphins were released into pain-related areas of the brain and their sensitivity to the pain actually decreased.

In another recent study[13], Harvard psychologist Ellen Langer studied hotel maids. She interviewed 84 hotel maids at seven different hotels about their exercise habits and found that two thirds did not exercise regularly and one-third did not exercise at all. Langer and

---

[11] Lanza and Berman, **Biocentrism: How Life and Consciousness Are the Keys to Understanding the True Nature of the Universe,** Ben Bella Books (2009).
[12] **Journal of Neuroscience** (August 24, 2005; 25:34)
[13] http://www.npr.org/templates/story/story.php?storyId=17792517

her student Alia Crum told half the women that in their work at the hotels cleaning fifteen guestrooms each, they were exceeding the surgeon general's recommendations for physical activity. A month later Langer and Crum found that the group that had been educated about their activity had level had lost an average of two pounds and saw a 10-point drop in their blood pressure. Neither group had changed their exercise habits.

There is a negative effect that is observed when negative beliefs are applied, and that is called the "nocebo" effect. New Scientist, an online web magazine, reported[14] that Sam Shoeman, diagnosed with end-stage liver cancer in the 1970s, was told by his doctors that he would die within months. He died within the prescribed time frame, but an autopsy discovered that the doctors were wrong: the cancer was tiny and had not metastasized. He died from *believing* that he had cancer.

This same article reported that a study in the Journal of the American Medical Association examined fifteen trials involving thousands of patients who were prescribed either beta blockers or a placebo. Both groups reported comparable side effects such as fatigue, depression and sexual symptoms.

Despite this obvious link between the mind and the body, few studies have been done to prove its significance and many scientists continue to resist the idea that the mind and consciousness can create our reality as well as affect our health. But this is beginning to change. Through the work of Dr. Bruce Lipton and others, the power of the belief systems held in the conscious mind to create change in both our inner and outer worlds is beginning to be recognized by more and more scientific experts, and new fields of study are beginning to arise.

Epigenetics is a new field that studies the interrelationship between the environment and DNA. Scientists at Duke University have demonstrated that "behaviors or environmental exposure of

---

[14] Helen Filcher, "The Science of Voodoo: When mind attacks body," in New Scientist online magazine, May 13, 2009, issue 2708.

any sort can silence or activate a gene without altering its genetic code in any way." [15] According to Fred Tyson, Ph.D., a researcher at NIEHS that worked on this project: "'Each nutrient, each interaction, each experience can manifest itself through biochemical changes that ultimately dictate gene expression, whether at birth or 40 years down the road."[16]

Research from the Heart Math Institute on something they call "heart intelligence" has shown that

> the electromagnetic signals generated by the heart have the capacity to affect others around us. Our data indicate that one person's heart signal can affect another's brainwaves, and that heart-brain synchronization can occur between two people when they interact. Finally, it appears that as individuals increase psychophysiological coherence, they become more sensitive to the subtle electromagnetic signals communicated by those around them. Taken together, these results suggest that cardioelectromagnetic communication may be a little-known source of information exchange between people, and that this exchange is influenced by our emotions.[17]

In this way, we absorb a great deal of data about the world we live in through our contact with others, including our beliefs and the very construct of our reality.

Scientists have known for quite some time that an electromagnetic energy field surrounds the human body, but new research shows that the brain and the heart also elicit their own energy fields, and that the heart has an electromagnetic field that is much stronger than that of the brain. The signatures of the rhythms of the electromagnetic field of the heart are altered as the emotions experienced by the individual change. Negative emotions create an erratic and incoherent wave pattern, and harmonious emotions such

---

[15] Newsletter, DukeHealth.org, http://www.dukehealth.org/HealthLibrary/News/9322, October 25, 2005.
[16] Ibid.
[17] Science of the Heart, Institute of Heartmath website:
http://www.heartmath.org/research/science-of-the-heart-head-heart-interactions.html

as love create a smooth and coherent pattern. Scientists call this "cardiac coherence" and this information is being used to develop new treatments for stress-related disease.

All of this new scientific research is proving what the ancient wisdom schools taught for thousands of years: that the human body and spirit are intricately connected with the world around us, and that the impetus of creation passes in both directions. Not only does our world affect our experience, but we affect our world as well. As Deepak Chopra wrote:

> We are not onlookers peering into the unified field of separate, objective reality - we are the unified field. We can reach beyond the physical body and extend the influence of intelligence. Every thought you are thinking creates a wave in the unified field. It ripples through all the layers of intellect, mind, senses, and matter, spreading out in wider and wider circles.
>
> You are like a light radiating not photons but consciousness. As they radiate, your thoughts have an effect on everything. Your relationship to life is the same as that of one cell to your whole body. One cell can talk to your whole body. One cell can influence your whole body. You can talk to the whole of life - influence the whole of life. The whole of life is as alive as we are. The distinction between 'in here' and 'out there' is a false one - as if the heart disregarded the skin because it was not on the inside.[18]

When Deepak Chopra wrote these words back in 1990 these concepts were considered on the fringe of science. Now scientists have caught

---

[18] Deepak Chopra, **Quantum Healing: Exploring the frontiers of mind/body medicine**, Bantam Books, 1990, p. 203.

up with the ancient wisdom which teaches all life is interconnected, and that we have the power to create change in our world.

This power of creation begins with our beliefs.

Chapter Four:
What are beliefs?

Beliefs are ideas that we hold as true. Our beliefs construct the basis of our reality with varying levels of intensity and fervor, and we are more attached to some beliefs than others. Some of these beliefs have to do with the way the Universe works. Some are religious beliefs. In any event, a belief is an idea to which we are particularly attached.

Some beliefs are with us from birth, and we can usually see those embedded in the birthchart. If someone is born with Pluto conjunct the Moon, they will have a predisposition to *believe* that life and security (Moon) is inherently dangerous (Pluto). With Jupiter conjunct the Sun there may be a belief from birth that their essential Self (Sun) is important and can do anything (Jupiter).

Some beliefs are instilled in us from childhood. "Everyone in this family has allergies." "You will never amount to anything." "Your sister is the pretty one." If we don't already have a predisposition to such a belief it will be easier for us to resist it and change it later in our lives as our circumstances change.

Some beliefs are more changeable than others. Some of our beliefs have to do with our changing moods and tastes, such as "I don't like strawberries." A belief that people of another religion are dangerous can change if we spend time with those people and find that we have more in common than we thought.

While many of our beliefs live in the conscious mind, many beliefs are submerged into the subconscious and lurk there where they are more difficult to access.

A belief originates as a thought which is analyzed by the brain. In doing so, neural pathways are formed as the data passes through the brain, and additional cells are imprinted with this data. The conscious mind interprets the data, attaching an emotion to it depending upon our past experience and our needs at the time, and this is what converts the thought to a belief. The belief is then stored in the subconscious mind where it can be accessed later by the conscious mind in order to assess the validity of future data.

The emotion that is stored as belief in the subconscious mind carries a vibrational frequency that has a magnetic quality and attracts thoughts and experiences of a like frequency. In the subtle realm of experience, this magnetism draws the experiences to us that

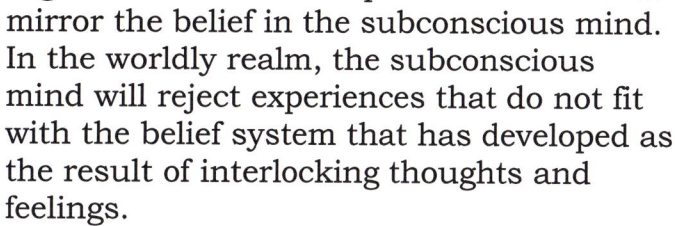

mirror the belief in the subconscious mind. In the worldly realm, the subconscious mind will reject experiences that do not fit with the belief system that has developed as the result of interlocking thoughts and feelings.

The beliefs in the subconscious mind hold more power than our conscious mind, since the subconscious controls nearly 90% of our thoughts. Conflicts between the subconscious and the conscious mind can result in behavior that sabotages our hopes and dreams.

If on the one hand you want to be a well-known public speaker, but have a subconscious belief that it is dangerous to be seen or visible, that will make it difficult for you to achieve your goal of helping thousands of people to change their own lives. If you consciously desire to be in a relationship, but subconsciously believe that relationships will stifle your ability to express yourself, you will repeatedly sabotage your relationships to protect your freedom.

In order to truly transform our lives, we must discover the subconscious beliefs that lie at the core of our psyche, and work with them so that they will permit change at the conscious level. For our friend from the example above who believes that life is inherently dangerous to create a life that brings a sense of freedom and adventure, we will need to first work through the belief system that instills such fear and keeps him locked into a life that is safe but dull.

Setting positive intentions and repeating affirmations *can* produce an effect, but until we resolve the conflicts created by the internal subconscious belief systems are not likely to create permanent change. We must work at the level of the *core beliefs*, the beliefs that compose the foundation of our reality and which limit the extent to which our reality can be transformed.

Although beliefs make up our sense of reality, they are not real. They are simply ideas that are attached to emotions that we *decide* are true. Some of our beliefs are supportive and harmonious with our Truth and the unfolding of our inner world. However, other beliefs create negativity and fear that hold us back. We didn't attach ourselves to negative beliefs because we are bad or deficient in some way. We created them to protect ourselves from harm, disappointment or danger.

Beliefs are simply habits of thinking that can be changed by introducing new habits and new ideas to form the basis of our reality. A belief that the Pope is infallible may serve us well in our early days as acolytes in the Church, but later in life we may decide to change this belief to one that offers us more freedom and the ability to make choices. In the same way, a negative belief that life is inherently dangerous can also be changed.

In order to change our world, we need to know what is driving us. Take a few moments right now to examine your own belief systems. What thoughts and ideas create the foundation of *your* world?

Chapter Five:
Visioncrafting in a financial crisis

In January of 2008 Pluto left the optimistic and expansive sign of Sagittarius and entered Capricorn, the sign of contraction and discipline, ending the financial bubbles that had marked the previous 13 years since Pluto entered Sagittarius in 1995. During that time the financial and housing markets reached astounding proportions, fueled by "irrational exuberance" and a belief that expansion could continue indefinitely.

When Pluto was in Sagittarius, between 1995 and 2008, this process of optimism creating abundance, which is after all a Sagittarian expansionist theme, became corrupted and rather than a healthy balance of optimism fueling production, we had an economy that was based on sheer optimism and speculation.

The globalization that spread like wildfire under Pluto in Sagittarius (the expansion of Sagittarius also includes travel and exploration of foreign cultures) caused the loss of over 3 million jobs in the United States. It can be argued that this contraction in the United States produced the expansion of the economies of China and India among others, but the point here is that this contraction of the US economy was not reflected in the "relentless optimism" as I called it that we saw here in the US. As a result, the economy became overinflated and the bubble has now burst and is slowly deflating.

This deflationary period is a natural one, but if we don't understand the underlying reality we can become fearful and panicky, particularly if we lose our job. If we aren't careful we can get caught in a spiral of despair that becomes a self-fulfilling prophecy as our belief that the economy is crashing creates that reality in our own lives. Sometimes our personal planetary cycles, especially if we are being visited by Saturn or Pluto, make it easy to slip into a gloom from which it is difficult to escape.

It is during these times that it's particularly important to focus on the positive and create strong intentions for the life that you want. It's easy to be positive when life is going great, but when we've lost our job, or our parent has died, or our spouse has left us and taken all of our money - those are times that truly test our faith in life. Focusing on the positive does not mean ignoring the negative. It does not mean slapping on a happy face and avoiding real problems that affect us. But it does mean a willingness to look for the door that is opening as one closes, and to know that we CAN create a life of prosperity and joy.

One thing I have found in these difficult times is that the abundance experience is not necessarily found in the sources from which we expect it. We may not find a job in the field for which we were trained. We may have to give up a dream from our past that we have held for so many years. But there are alternatives that will feed our souls in a way that is greater than anything we could have imagined, and provide the same or better prosperity than anything we could have imagined.

Chapter Six:
What is a life of abundance?

Abundance is the natural state of the Universe.

*It is the free flow of energy,
which is literally all around us in infinite supply.*

It is available to us whenever we are open to receiving it.

Most of us who live in Western civilizations consider abundance to be the same as prosperity: financial wealth. But is financial prosperity enough to give us the experience of an abundant life?

Literature around the world is full of tales of wealthy people who led miserable lives, such as Ebenezer Scrooge from Charles Dickens' *A Christmas Carol*. Scrooge has plenty of money but lives an isolated and miserable life until the Christmas ghosts teach him the lesson of gratitude and openness that is the foundation of the principle of abundance. Stories abound of the terrible luck of lottery winners.

Abundance is the experience of plenty; it is an experience of openness and giving as well as receiving. Prosperity and financial wealth is part of it; but so is having an abundance of time to enjoy and appreciate our lives . The ability to receive love is an abundant experience. So is the peace of a strong connection to Spirit.

Our entire economic system is based on perception: when consumer confidence is high, people buy stuff and go on vacation. The more they spend, the busier the factories and service industries are. The more the factories produce and the busier the service industries are, the more jobs there are for workers and the more stuff those workers can then buy. Meanwhile, investors buy stock in these companies and the stock goes up based on the perception that the companies are making more money.

It often takes just one event to reverse the trend, and fear is the emotion that drives recession and contraction in the economy. When people are afraid, they stay home from the mall and the airports. The economy contracts and the stock market falls, and everyone has less.

When our life is abundant, we find ourselves in balance in all ways including the giving and receiving of resources. We experience the satisfaction of having plenty so we are able to give to others without depleting our own supplies. We feel energized and able to maintain a positive outlook, confident in the power of Life to bestow blessings upon us.

Before we can begin to create a vision for a newly abundant experience of life we need to become fully aware of the possibilities. Financial prosperity, certainly – but where else could your life be more joyful, more comfortable, and more supportive of your dreams?

Perhaps you would like a better relationship with your partner or your children. Time to write that book you've always dreamed of. The courage to take a solo vacation. To play the piano again. To work at a job where you are respected and valued. More friends, or more satisfying friendships. A spiritual community. A home that supports and nurtures you.

Take a moment now to write down your first thoughts about areas where your life could expand into a more abundant experience. Time, health, love, home, music, creativity, joy, success, recognition, family, safety, fun, spiritual experience ... where can you find an opening to receive more in your life?

Chapter Seven:
What abundance is NOT...

*'Americans excel at making a living
but fail at making a life.'*
Dr. David Myers

Abundance is NOT the accumulation of wealth to the exclusion of joy and peace in our life. Working 100 hours a week to achieve a career goal may bring success and financial rewards, but it will come at the expense of a satisfying personal life. Scrimping and deprivation may bring security in retirement, but it may bring with it a persistent fear of loss. Hoarding is an experience of contraction that is based in fear.

The principle of abundance is based on trust and faith; a process that for many of us takes regular practice to accomplish! Therefore, any desire that is motivated by fear will not bring an experience of abundance.

Perhaps we are afraid to be alone and we seek a life partner to make us feel more secure: a goal such as this will not bring an experience of abundance into our life. On the other hand, an intention to bring love into our life in the form of a partner with whom we can share a loving relationship and build security together will result in an abundance of love in our life.

When we lack trust and faith in our life, we grasp and cling, fearing that there will not be enough. When we have brought abundance into our life we are able to open our hands and hearts to that which is given. When there is more room to receive, we are able to receive more. The closed hand can receive only so much.

Abundance is also not the fulfillment of endless desire. "I would be happy if only I had a Mercedes." "If I only made a lot of money, then I would be happy." "When I have a child, then I will truly be happy." "When I eat that chocolate dessert, then I'll really be happy." The idea that anything in the material world will bring fulfillment at the soul level is a fallacy that must be eliminated in order to achieve true abundance. True abundance, as the experience of fulfillment, contentment and joy, occurs whether or not worldly desires are realized. The desire nature is endlessly hungry and once one desire is obtained the hunger shifts to the next object.

Can you identify times when attempts to increase your abundance in one area of your life brought you out of balance in another? We don't want to dwell on the negative for too long, but looking at past errors can help us to identify strategies for change. Perhaps you gambled at a casino and lost your tuition money. Maybe you pursued a partner who later turned out to be a cad. Or gave 100 hours a week to a job with a good salary but lost touch with your family. What are some examples of situations and experiences in which you achieved your desires and then discovered they were not all that you had hoped?

_____

_____

_____

_____

Chapter Eight:
Principles of abundance

---

1. We create our own reality based on our belief systems.

     As we discovered in Chapter Four, all of us have powerful belief systems that drive us. When I work with astrology clients I hear these belief systems in action. "I could never run my own business, I'm not smart enough." "Whenever I fall in love I always end up hurt." "No matter how hard I work there's never enough money." These are tapes that we run over and over again in our mind until we are absolutely convinced that they are True with a capital T.

     Belief systems define the limits of our experience. They help us to develop a sense of meaning in life, as in theological belief systems. Sometimes we inherit them from our parents or are siblings, and sometimes they are indoctrinated into us. But more often we create belief systems for ourselves. We often develop these belief systems as a reaction to events that cause pain, and they are intended to protect us. If we know we're going to fail, we won't attempt to succeed so we won't feel the pain of failure. These beliefs become part of our very sense of Self and we may feel threatened at the hint of change.

Because these beliefs are so entrenched, we magnetize situations and events in our life that will reinforce them.

Even though we may dislike our belief systems, they are comfortable and familiar to us. Sometimes comfort drives us deeper and deeper into the rut of dysfunction. We may think we want success but if we have a belief system of fear we will be more comfortable with failure.

It often takes a conscious application of Will and intention to make a change in our belief system that will change our life. This is called a "Paradigm Shift" in the world of science because an entire world view and all of its implications changes when an established scientific theory is challenged.

Many books on prosperity consciousness and abundance tell us to change these belief systems, but they don't provide a method for accomplishing that difficult task. In these pages we will begin to recognize our belief systems, identify the ones that are holding us back, and create a new world view so that we can experience our own Paradigm Shift into a new reality!

Take the beliefs that you wrote down in Chapter Four and list each one here. Consider each one closely. Where did it originate? Is this a pattern that runs in your family? Did you adopt it later in life? Does it carry an emotional charge, and if so what is the emotion that accompanies it? If it is a negative belief, what purpose does it serve? How does it hinder or limit you? If it is a positive belief, does it adequately express the person that you are today? That you would like to be tomorrow?

This exercise encompasses both the negative and the positive beliefs because later on we will use both to create your powerful new visions. Both are important and make up the foundation of the beliefs that are creating our present reality. In order to change our reality, our beliefs will need to evolve and transform. For now though, don't judge any of these beliefs – just write them down. We'll work to transform them later in the book.

2. That which we focus on expands and gains more power.

If you've ever experienced an anxiety attack, you know the power of fixation. The more you fixate on your fear the more it increases and gains power, and this is true for anything that we give our attention to. As we focus our consciousness on a thought or idea it increase in authority and becomes our reality.

This works for changing the behavior of others as well as our own behavior. The more we focus on the bad behavior of our children and spouses, the worse that behavior becomes. Focusing instead on good behavior brings about much more promising results.

Our thoughts possess energy of their own that feed this process of expansion and increase in power, and this process works just as well for positive thoughts as it does for negative ones. The groundbreaking work of Bruce Lipton PhD, whose earlier cited book **The Biology of Belief** is highly recommended, reveals that the subconscious mind actually controls the body, turning genes for specific behaviors on and off. As noted earlier, the new science called "biocentrism" has shown that human thought and consciousness creates the world around us. So science and spiritual philosophy are beginning to join forces in new and powerful ways.

Can you identify experiences where changing your focus has changed your reality, in both positive and negative ways?

_____

_____

_____

_____

3. Abundance is available in infinite supply.

One fear that we sometimes have is that if our life is more abundant, someone else will suffer as a result. Nothing could be further from the truth! Faith in the unlimited supply of universal gifts is a fundamental principle of abundance. A belief in scarcity leads us to fear that if we have more, someone else will have less. Perhaps a deep sense of guilt has been instilled in us from childhood and we feel we are not deserving of pleasure and comfort, or it may be that our personality is wired to be more of a giver than one who receives. While this is a noble characteristic, we cannot truly give when our own resources are limited.

Take a moment to repeat this, out loud: *Abundance is available in infinite supply.*

As long as the flow of resources of all kinds does not become blocked and stagnant, there is no end to the supply of the gifts of the Universe. It is true that greed and endless consumption on the part of some does create a shortage in the lives of others. But greed and a hunger for acquisition does not constitute an abundant life; rather, this kind of greedy consumption typically arises from a hole in the heart and a deep sense of lack in the soul.

A simple experience in the power of the Universe to create abundance in our lives and the lives of those around us brings good things into our life, and also gives us the opportunity to share this goodness with others in our family, our community, and our world.

Which leads us very nicely to the next principle…

4. Giving and receiving must occur in balance to ensure the continuous flow of energy.

I have friends who are firmly entrenched in poverty because they persist in giving away more resources than they have. "I spend this money to make way for the new money," they say, thinking that this affirmation alone will be enough to build prosperity and wealth. But we must cultivate a balance in all things in order to achieve a truly abundant experience of our lives.

When I first began the process of creating an abundant life I became very good at making money, but because I gave it all away I wasn't experience the abundance for which I had hoped. Many of us have not yet resolved our underlying sense of guilt or lack of self-worth that enables us to feel deserving of the material and emotional wealth that is available to us. As we begin to recognize and outgrow these old belief systems we will become better able to balance the ebb and flow of resources in a way that permits growth and continued expansion.

On the other hand, a greedy need for acquisition will stop the flow of energy and prevent an experience of abundance. As we have noted previously, greed is an experience of contraction that is based in fear and keeps us from experiencing the expansive trust and faith that will assist in creation of the life that we have dreamed of.

Now it's time to take some notes. Can you identify messages that you have internalized about there being not "enough"? Are there areas of your life where you fear that you will always be deprived? Where in your life is the flow of giving and receiving out of balance, and where have you succeeded in creating that balance?

_____

_____

_____

5. Gratitude for what we have expands our ability to receive.

When we experience gratitude we open our hearts and minds and counteract the contraction of fear and doubt. A gratitude practice is a very useful tool. It is human nature not to pay attention to the good things in our life and to take them for granted; a daily review of the things for which we are grateful can help to refocus our attention and help us to build the positive attitude that is the foundation of transmuting the base metal of our life into the gold of transformation and actualization.

Marcus Tulius Cicero said, back in ancient Rome, "Gratitude is not only the greatest of virtues but the parent of all others." Gratitude for what we are given is the single key that turns prosperity and wealth into a true experience of abundance.

Gratitude is an emotion that is felt primarily in the heart center. On a mundane level a practice of gratitude helps us to maintain perspective about our lives. On a more esoteric level, gratitude opens the heart center which helps us to ascend from the ego into an experience of divine love and consciousness. This openness helps to unlock the blocks of fear which opens the door to transformation.

Gratitude also helps us to expand beyond judgment and restriction. When we approach the experiences of our life with a sense of gratitude, it becomes much easier for us to see every experience as an opportunity for growth and transformation rather than a burden. It is impossible to be a victim when we are grateful for what we have been given.

What are you grateful for in your life? Loved ones, events, coincidences, experiences, talents, acquaintances – list as many as you can in order to continue the process of opening the heart and expanding the sense of possibility.

6. *Holding on is the result of a belief in shortage.*

Letting the energy flow around our experiences enhances our joy and opens the doors to new experiences and greater expansion.

Often we become stuck in a situation because we fear that there are no other options. We stay in a relationship that is dissatisfying or abusive because we are afraid "no one better will come along." We stay in a job where we are endlessly criticized because we are afraid that we are too old to be hired somewhere else.

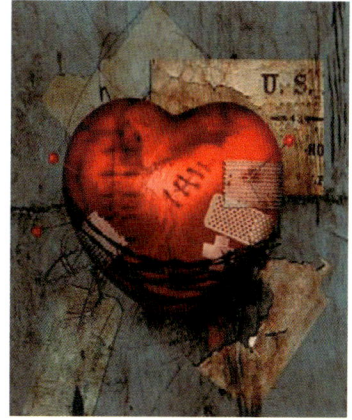

Sometimes our desire for security and our fear of change keeps us from believing that we **can** have what we desire. It feels safer to remain with that which is known than to take the risk of the unknown. We fear that we will end up with nothing.

The principle of scarcity cannot exist simultaneously with the principle of abundance as it is based on the fear which stops the flow. In order to make the shift required to open up a life of greater abundance, the principle of scarcity must be abandoned. This can be a difficult step to take as it requires a leap of faith and takes us far from our comfort zone, but for that reason it is one of the most powerful things that we can do to change our life. By removing ourselves from an experience that is limiting or harmful, we send a powerful message to the Universe that we are ready for an experience that will be supportive and joyful.

If we are not ready to take such a drastic step we can begin by simply opening to the possibility of change in our situation. Letting go of our attachment to the situation in which we find ourselves, and opening up to the possibility of something new and liberating, can be enough to open the door.

About faith: Letting go requires a certain amount of faith. Faith in what, you might ask? That depends upon your own theology of life; the belief systems that give your life meaning. In life, bad and difficult things often happen. Our desires are often frustrated and our lives frequently take turns that we had not anticipated and would not have chosen. At these times we may feel we can no longer have faith in our God, or the Universal Perfection of All Things.

But we may not be looking at the whole picture. In my work with clients I have seen over and over that hidden in the most difficult and painful situations there is a seed of something new. Sometimes my clients just need a hand to hold so that they can take that step out of their small perspective. Once this new seed has an opportunity to blossom, magic begins to happen and their life expands with a brand new beauty.

Think back to times when you have felt stuck in your life, and see if you can remember opportunities that were available to you once you freed yourself from those situations.

_____

_____

_____

_____

_____

_____

_____

_____

_____

7. Each moment offers the freedom for conscious choice.

The alchemical process by which we change our belief systems is not one that takes place only in defined spaces. We have the freedom every moment of the day to make a conscious choice about where we will put our attention and how we will frame our thoughts and the events of our life that accompany them.

The goal here is not the repression of negativity – each thought that enters our mind has something to teach us about ourselves and the way we interact with the world. If we can take the time to observe those thoughts that hold us firmly within our old belief systems and then consciously reframe them into a positive expression of who we really are, we will be well on our way to manifesting deep change in our lives.

Notice that this principle uses the word "choice." *Choice* is a very different concept from *decision*. The word *choice* means to make a selection from a variety of options and is from the Latin root meaning "to taste." When we make a conscious choice, we realize that we have options. Choice empowers us; it offers us an array of options from which we can choose one, and we have the opportunity to change our mind later.

Think about the difference between "I choose to quit smoking," and "I decided to quit smoking." The idea that we *choose* empowers us because we understand that we have a choice.

The word *decision* is from the Latin root meaning "to cut off." When we make a decision, we cut off other options. When we decide, we make a judgment about the issue and reach a conclusion. It is a mental action that does not imply the empowerment to create our reality.

The art of becoming ever more present in our day to day experience is a wonderful tool in this work and in any kind of personal development. As we learn to become an observer of our thoughts, we become better able to make the kinds of choices that are needed to inspire change in our lives. When we react from subconscious emotion we are the victims of the mind, rather than co-conscious creators with the power to make choices.

Later in this program you will learn specific tools for doing just that. Meanwhile, begin to pay closer attention to the stream of your thoughts during the day and watch where those thoughts take you. See if you can put your thoughts on pause when negativity begins to cloud your vision, and just observe those thoughts and the emotions that come with them. Often when I work with clients they will want to scold themselves when their thoughts turn negative. This is the wrong choice! Instead, make the choice to turn around and reframe the negative into a positive viewpoint.

Take a moment now to think about decisions that you have made through reacting to an event rather than a choice. See if there are areas in your life that would benefit from a more conscious approach. What does the idea of *choice* mean to you?

_____

_____

_____

_____

_____

_____

_____

8. Conscious creation requires a balance between will and surrender

When working with Intention and Will there is a danger that we will fall prey to the belief that we possess the ultimate control over our destiny. Although we can transform our thought patterns and achieve greater mastery over that destiny, the process is a co-creative one. Our partner is the Wisdom of Divine Intelligence.

Sometimes we simply do not get what we want or when we want it. This does not negate the power of the conscious mind to manifest the life of our dreams; it simply reminds us that there is a loving Higher Consciousness with a greater perspective and wisdom.

All of us on Planet Earth have celestial teachers and guides that assist us in our evolutionary journey. Perhaps we call this Intelligence God, or Spirit, or Jesus, or Buddha. Perhaps we prefer to think of a personal god such as Lakshmi or Kuan Yin, or the face of our Guru or other spiritual teachers. Some of us connect to what we call our "higher selves." These teachers guide us with the greater perspective that goes beyond time and space, and possess wisdom that we with our limited view are unable to achieve.

The understanding that astrology provides can help us through difficult times and give us perspective so that we avoid becoming discouraged when our lives are not working out as we hoped. Sometimes we are undergoing planetary transits of Saturn that create blocks or delays in the fulfillment of our desires, and in those cases we need to learn patience and the beauty of hard work and planning. Or a transit of Pluto may destroy a relationship that we thought was perfect, and we need to learn the value of letting go of that which the Universe determines is standing in the way of our ultimate happiness. Or perhaps a bountiful Jupiter transit has filled us with confidence and we lose all of our money at the gambling table.

If we try to manifest a desire that is not for our ultimate good, our spiritual guidance will not permit this desire to manifest. Therefore, as we begin to create a new vision for a more abundant experience in our life we must incorporate a willingness to surrender to the wisdom of that Greater Intelligence to provide circumstances that are superior to that which we can imagine for ourselves.

There are other factors too that sometimes keep us from achieving our dreams. Often we have desires that are not in harmony with each other, or wishes that are not in harmony with our core values. For example, one part of us may want to quit our job and stay home with children, and another part may want to build a real estate empire. The difficulty here is not that so much that the two experiences are out of alignment; it is more that the values that underlie the experiences cannot coexist. We want to stay at home to retreat from the world and nurture our children, but another part of us wants to experience the creative mastery of achievement through business. At that point the Divine Intelligence that guides us will step in and help us to create a life experience that synchronizes our desires in a way that is most helpful to our ultimate soul growth.

In other situations we may desire a certain life path, but there may be an alternative of which we are not yet aware that is for our ultimate highest good. In those situations our desire may not be fulfilled and we will need to hold that sense of faith that the Universe is acting to create exactly the best situation for us that may be beyond anything we can imagine.

For example, you may want to begin a new career as a massage therapist, but perhaps through taking some additional courses you discover an entirely new modality that takes you in a different direction entirely. Or perhaps you have a dream of moving to Hawaii, but then you discover a magical town in Florida where the perfect opportunities await you. It is nearly always true that when every door we knock on fails to open, there is another option on the horizon that will take us in a different option. This is where faith comes in.

Think for a moment about your goals, dreams and wishes. How specific are they? Can you expand your thinking to allow for the wisdom of the Universe to intervene?

Chapter Nine:
The crafting of wishes

The Magician, by Willow Arlenea

'If you don't have an intention, you live your life by default.'

Now we come to the fun part! Here is where we get to explore the art of Wishcraft. We will begin by looking at all of the areas of our life and simply listing everything that we would like to change in these areas. Give yourself the freedom here to really think about your life; what brings you contentment and where you feel you need more in order to experience a sense of plenty. The language in these pages is not important – this exercise is designed as an opportunity to become more informed about your life and how you feel about it.

Under each category just start writing. What would you like to improve? What are you happy with? What would you like to bring into your life that you don't have now? What would you like to eliminate?

Take plenty of time – in my workshops we spend at least a half hour on this section. The more time you give this process the deeper into your subconscious you will travel and the more creative energy you will generate.

The categories are meant only as a guide for your exploration process; don't worry about what goes into which category. You will note that the categories begin on the inside and work their way out. Some of us will have an easier time with some categories than others. If you are already successful in your business but want to create a life that you enjoy, you will want to focus on the "Fun" category. If you can't pay your rent, the "Money" category will be the most important for now. Some categories will be more important to you, but don't neglect the others. One important facet of this exercise is to recognize the need for balance in all areas of life.

Self: This category includes anything that has to do with personal development or self-improvement. Personal habits such as quitting smoking, diet and exercise fall under this category, or attributes that we want to develop such as greater courage or open-mindedness. Any personality characteristics that we want to change, such as being friendlier and less critical, or even just laughing more and being more accepting of others. Things that we do to take care of ourselves or to develop a skill or talent also fit in this category. Learning a language or practicing a musical instrument can also be included here.

Spirit: This section is for deepening our connection to Spirit. This can be through a regular practice or prayer, taking classes or learning new skills, expanding our spiritual understanding, attending regular services or joining a community. Maybe you seek to find more faith or learn to listen to your own inner voice. Perhaps you want to deepen your yoga practice, or develop your own intuition. Receive more wisdom from your dreams, or enhance your psychic abilities. This is also the section for creating a sacred space in your home and office, and to bring more Spirit into your marriage or any kind of relationship.

Heart: In this section we find all kinds of relationships including those with parents, spouse, friends, children, pets. Here is where we open our heart to love in new ways, or attract new relationships. Perhaps we want to improve our relationships, or leave one. Although we cannot set intentions for others, in this section go ahead and include the details of any changes you desire in your personal connections. Later on we will see how to create the vision so that it does not interfere with the free will of those around us.

Home: Here you can list any of your desires regarding your home or the place that you live. This includes buying or selling a home, finding the right community or neighborhood, redecorating, completing home improvement projects, enhancing of the beauty of the outdoors of your home. You can also choose here to enhance your housekeeping and bring the joy of community into your home. If you long for a home at the beach or a second home in the mountains, here's the place to list that wish.

Fun: What kind of fun experiences do you want to bring into your life? Here we include vacations, more time for play with our children, travel to new places, attending museums and other fun places with friends and family. Sports and creative pursuits such as art and music can go here if they are strictly for fun; if there is a goal attached, such as "have a gallery show" or "play with a band," you may want to include that wish in the "Accomplishment" section.

This is a difficult section for some people. "Fun? What's that? I'm too busy trying to hold everything together to have fun." That's when we need fun the most. Enjoying our life is the lubricant that keeps our lives running smoothly and opens the door to happiness. No matter how busy you are, or how intense your focus on your goals, *always* make room for the Fun section.

Accomplishment: Here is where you list your dreams for success and a sense of achievement. This includes success in business, publishing a book, completing your education or taking classes or other accreditations. Perhaps you have a project that you would like to complete; list it here. If recognition by others and some sort of status in the world is important to you, list it here. Do not judge your desire for success and recognition if you have it; it was planted in you for a reason! This is no time for false modesty, so be as clear as possible.

Things: This is the section for our "toys": cars, computers, gadgets, jewelry, hot tubs, boats. List as much detail as possible: the brand, the way it looks, the color, etc. Include details about how you feel when you have these things and how they help you in your life. For example, perhaps the boat provides an opportunity for you and your family to feel closer. The hot tub offers a chance to relax. Jewelry helps you to feel beautiful, and gadgets help you to organize your life.

Money: Last but not least! Use real numbers here, and allow yourself to expand your thinking. Do not find excuses to think small. Yes, we are in a recession, but that does not have to affect your personal financial situation! Think about actual dollar figures, and write them down. How much income do you need to feel secure? How much in savings? What about retirement? How will you feel when you have it? How about donating to others or setting up a foundation? Perhaps your financial situation is sound and money is not a concern to you; in that case you may be more interested in finding ways to put your money to work to change the world.

Fill up these pages as much as you can. This is an exercise in expanding your vision of what is actually possible, so think big and don't second guess yourself. When we create your vision statements we will be working only with the ten or fifteen items that are most important, but over time you will want to come back to this list and add or subtract as your life begins to change.

Self

Spirit

Heart

Home

Fun

Accomplishment _____

Things _____
_____
_____

Money

Chapter Ten:
Obstacles which keep us from realizing our dreams

Take your list, and consider every item. What do you think has kept you from achieving this goal? What are the messages your mind sends you about whether or not this goal can come true?

Often we are blocked by certain belief systems that we reinforce daily by the way we think about things – by the "tapes" that we run in our head. "Who do I think I am to think I could be successful?" "If I am no longer a victim, who will take care of me?" "Why would anyone love me?" "If I am wealthy, my family will reject me." "If I have good things in my life, other people will suffer."

The fact is that even in these difficult economic times, opportunities are everywhere. We are creating our reality right now, without even thinking about it. Every time we tell ourselves "I can't," we reinforce this fact for ourselves.

The Visioncrafting process simply reverses the negative beliefs that have become truths for us, and creates new truths which support the more expansive life that we are seeking. Using this process, we create intentions and ask the Universe in its wisdom to provide what is needed for our continued growth and fulfillment. But first we must unwind the patterning that has brought us the dissatisfaction that we want to change.

For example, I used to always say "I don't have any money." When someone would invite me to a movie, I would say "I don't have any money." When I went shopping, I would say "I don't have any money." Over time I learned that every time I repeated this mantra I was keeping financial prosperity from becoming a reality. I was making plenty of money, but I never had any in my bank account. When I began this Visioncrafting process, I started to say "There is always plenty of money to do anything that I want to do." Suddenly I found there was cash in my wallet, a previously unheard of event!

In Chapter Four you made a list of some of the patterns of belief that are keeping you from living the life of your dreams. Here we are going to focus on the negative beliefs – but just for a short time. Over the next few days, listen to the tapes that you play and the messages that you give yourself every day. Learn to pay attention when you say things like "I always…" or "I never…" which are signals that this is an entrenched belief. For example, "I always screw up my relationships" or "I will never learn to play the piano."

In the next section, write out as many of these negative core beliefs that you can find. Once you have your list of negative beliefs, transform them in the following section into positive and empowering beliefs that reverse the negative ideas from the past. Using the example above, "I always screw up my relationships" would then become "I always manage my relationships well. " "I am too old to find a new job" is transformed into "My exceptional skills and terrific attitude are valued by employers everywhere, and I have my choice of wonderful jobs in locations that are perfect for me."

Try to develop a habit of listening to your mind's messages. If you hear one of these negative beliefs slip in to your consciousness stop yourself immediately and rewind the tape. Then speak the new one right away, out loud if possible. Eventually, I promise, it will become a habit that will transform your life!

My old negative beliefs that are now in the past:

My new positive beliefs:

Additional notes:

Chapter Eleven:
Creating a new vision

Scientists have discovered that our thoughts actually control our DNA, but the conscious mind operates less than 5% of the time (*Bruce Lipton, <u>The Biology of Belief</u>.*) By creating powerful vision statements which we repeat regularly, we retrain our thought patterns and create neurological changes in our subconscious belief systems. Through a daily practice of reframing our previous negative beliefs into beliefs that empower us, we transform the way we approach each choice we make in a way that transforms every event in our lives.

This is not the same as positive thinking or affirmations. An example of positive thinking would be, "I will get this job." Or "I know that I deserve love and accept it now." Positive thinking occurs at the level of the conscious mind, when the subconscious mind is operating 95% of our lives. Most affirmation practices operate at the level of positive thinking, but they do not delve into the subconscious to uncover the negative belief systems that are holding us back in order to retrain the brain into a completely new way of thinking.

Because the Visioncrafting process helps us to actually alter these core belief systems it has a powerful ability to make deep and lasting changes. It is most effective when used as a daily practice that incorporates several steps.

Vision Statements:

Creating powerful vision statements is the key to the Vision-crafting practice. A vision statement is similar to an affirmation, but it is more powerful because it actually replaces an outmoded belief system with a new one and retrains your subconscious mind. It also uses the power of your emotions and desires to motivate you to the action required to set your goals into motion and inspire change.

To begin, take the ten or fifteen most important things from the lists you made in the Crafting of Wishes section, and list them here. You may find that some of the wishes you listed are linked together; if so, go ahead and combine them. For example, if one of your wishes is to improve your relationship with your children and another one is to spend more time going to fun places with them, it would be natural to combine those two goals.

For now, just think about which of all of those items in your big list are most important, and see if there are any others that you can associate with your big items. For each item, go back to Chapter Ten where we transformed our negative beliefs, and see if any of these correspond to your important wishes. In the example above, perhaps the negative belief that has kept you from spending more time with your children is that you have a core belief that there's never enough time to enjoy yourself. If you see a belief like this, write it down next to your most important wishes.

There may not be an associated negative belief – it may just be that you have not been able to manifest a particular wish because you haven't assigned enough priority to it. This process will help you to elevate its status in your consciousness and focus more attention and intention, which will help you to achieve the wish.

So in this section, list your ten or fifteen most important items along with any associated negative beliefs that you come up with.

We're not concerned with the language here – we're just setting the stage and identifying what we have to work with. Write as much detail as possible about every item.

_____

_____

_____

_____

_____

_____

_____

_____

_____

_____

_____

_____

_____

Now we will begin to craft our Vision Statements. For each of your ten or fifteen most important items, don't write anything yet. Instead, begin by thinking about what your life will look like and feel like when that first wish has come true. Use the notes that you have written and the power of your emotions and imagination to shape a vision that is rich and colorful and inspiring to you.

To get an idea of how this works, let's start with your first wish. How do you feel when this wish has been achieved?

_____

_____

_____

_____

What does the picture in your mind look like? Describe it exactly.

_____

_____

_____

_____

_____

Now, if there is a fear or core belief that has kept you from realizing this wish in the past, let's address it. Use the skills that you learned earlier in this program and transform that belief into a positive one. Use words like "I easily and effortlessly," or "I feel comfortable and safe" in order to encourage your subconscious to move forward without fear or blockages.

For example, let's say that one of your wishes is to become a successful full-time fiction writer, and the block that you identified is a lack of time to write and a fear that you will not be able to support yourself. You will want to incorporate these identified problems into your vision in order to counteract them, by writing something like this: "I am easily able to schedule time to write my first book of fiction, and write 20 pages a day. The words come quickly and effortlessly, and the book is soon finished. It is well received by the agents who review it, and I am awarded an advance of $100,000. The book is a best-seller and provides an income to me of over $100,000 a year."

As you can see, this vision statement has incorporated the fears that have kept you from achieving this dream and made it a part of the intention. Without this part of the process, the subconscious blocks that have kept you from realizing your dreams will still be at work. In this way we don't try to ignore or avoid the negative beliefs, we actually transform them into a way of thinking that works FOR us.

When you are creating your vision statements, keep the following in mind:

- Use all of your senses to create the new vision. What does the scene look like? How do you feel in the new situation? Describe it as completely as you can. The more real you make your vision, the more quickly the changes will begin.

- Use positive language only, and language that energizes and inspires you. Examples: "I wake up every morning excited to be going to my new job..." or "I confidently walk into every speaking engagement, knowing that I have valuable insights to share."

- Use the context of the "present time" such as, "I am involved in a loving and balanced relationship"... "I feel comfortable and secure with $500,000 invested in my retirement account.

- Be as specific as possible, but leave room for guidance and inspiration. If you want to start a new career but don't know exactly what kind of job you want to do, think about what you want this new career to include. How do you want to feel when you're at work? What are the people you work with like? Do you work for a large company or at home? The Wisdom of the Universe will take care of the rest.

- ❖ Use words such as "the best possible…" or "exactly the right…" to allow room for divine intervention.

- ❖ Include language that makes it all happen easily, effortlessly, freely, and efficiently.

- ❖ Remember that you cannot set intentions for other people, only for yourself. When we want to change our relationships it is usually because we want to feel differently than we do presently. It is the *feeling* that is the most important thing, and that is what you want to focus on. In this situation, phrase your vision so that it is centered more about how you *feel* in the relationship than on the actual *behavior* of the other person.

    For example, instead of "George is a loving husband and always takes out the trash" you might say "I feel completely loved by George and know that I can rely on him to honor all of his responsibilities." In creating the experience of love and dependability in yourself, you will find ways to change the dynamics so that your desires can be achieved.

So take out some fresh sheets of paper and begin to craft your vision statements. Don't judge yourself. Just start writing – you can always change it later. In fact, as you work through this process over time you will likely change your vision statements many times. The most important thing is that these statements excite you and inspire you so that change can happen. Within your heart a little voice should say "YES!" as you read each statement. You may still hear a little nagging voice of negativity, but as long as your heart says "YES!" you are on the right track!

In the next section you will some examples to help you get started. But remember, what makes Visioncrafting uniquely powerful is that your vision statements are designed specifically for you in order to unite your subconscious and conscious mind. If you find an example in this section that works for you, that's wonderful! But be sure that it addresses your own fears and blocks so that you can move through them more quickly and easily and achieve your dreams with greater efficiency and ease.

Chapter Twelve:
Examples to help you get started

I accomplish my goals easily and I effortlessly manifest all that I wish for.

The power of the Visioncrafting process lies in the fact that each vision statement is designed especially for you to transform your own belief systems and give you a new way of looking at your world. Still, many of us have similar blocks and similar needs, and so I offer these examples from my client files to help you to get started.

If you use these statements, change the language as needed so that the result is a powerful statement that resonates for you completely. When you read these, you want to feel fantastic and inspired. There may be doubt that you can make these changes and that's ok. You don't have to believe that you can – you only have to do the practice. We'll talk more about that later. But during this portion of the process, just be sure that every statement that you add to your list feels right and is exciting and inspiring.

To feel more positive and balanced:

My life is filled with beautiful experiences, adventures and possibilities that make me happy. I am easily able to move through periods of emotional complexity and return to a state that is positive and optimistic.

I am easily able to maintain a healthy balance in life with work, play, study, rest, relationships – every aspect of my life is satisfying and joyous.

I allow the love of the Universe to flow through me, lifting my life to new realms of possibilities.

For more organization and to release clutter:

I keep my home and office beautifully organized and decorated. My car, work and living spaces are free from clutter and filled with items of beauty that make me feel at home and comfortable.

Clearing out the clutter in my home helps me to move through my life more freely. I easily decide what to keep and what to give away, and poor families are grateful to receive the items that I donate.

I easily let go of and release the things in my life that I no longer need because I fully recognize that in clearing out these things I am freeing myself to move forward into the light of a fresh new beginning.

To attract just the right relationship:

I am involved in a stable and loving relationship with a man who treasures my company and with whom I feel completely secure. He adores me and shows me that I am his top priority. We have fun together and enjoy each other's company. I have complete trust in this man and know that he will never hurt me. He is fully employed and earns more money than I do. He is successful and confident.
I feel confident and attractive in my ability to make good choices in my relationships with men, and to sustain these relationships over long periods of time.

I am involved with a kind and loving woman who shares my interests and values. She is compassionate and shows that she is interested in me. She takes initiative in the relationship and makes me feel special. I feel content and loved and the security I feel helps me to trust her.

I am in a loving and balanced relationship with an affectionate and caring man who respects me and is deeply committed to me. We enjoy spending time together, but we share the freedom to do anything that we want to do outside the relationship. He is my intellectual equal and is comfortable with my strength. He appreciates my unusual life and allows me to continue to grow and evolve both in the relationship and beyond it. He is willing to communicate with me so that our relationship becomes deeper and more true.

To improve your relationship or marriage:

I enjoy the commitment in my relationship, which fulfills me on the deepest level. I feel safe and comfortable, and our love is deep and offers the intense connection that I crave. We always make the time to nurture our relationship and love being together. I still have plenty of time to spend with my friends and on my own having new experiences that broaden my horizon.

I have a loving and balanced marriage, feeling cherished, adored, and emotionally secure. We feel safe with each other and the trust and love that we share opens our hearts to communicate easily. We love being together and enjoy doing fun things together. Our intimacy is passionate and exciting. I feel appreciated and valued by my husband.

I have a comfortable and secure relationship with my husband, who treats me with respect, kindness and love. We feel completely comfortable with each other and are able to talk through any problems that arise.

To attract more money and feel prosperous:

I feel comfortable and secure with $_____ in the bank, and easily pay all of my bills. There is always plenty of money to do whatever I want to do.

I am easily able to pay off all of my debts and remain debt free so that I can begin saving for a secure and happy retirement.

As I earn more wealth and become more financially secure, I am able to help to make a difference in people's lives by giving of both my time and my money.

To increase sales if you are self-employed:

I am excited by the opportunities that come my way and it's always fun for me to work with my clients. The sales come easily and close quickly, and my customers and clients are thrilled with my work and gladly refer their friends to me.

I effortlessly attract just the right clients who are open and have a sincere desire to grow, ready to begin their spiritual journey and evolution. My clients bloom and create more light in their lives. My work with them feels spacious and is full of divine love, service and beneficence. I feel energized and grateful for the opportunity to serve in this way.

To find a new career:

I have a successful career doing creative work that excites me and that I feel passionate about. My job is stable and secure, paying me over $150,000 a year with excellent benefits. I am worth every penny!

I have a fabulously successful business that fills me with joy and the knowledge that I am aligned with my true purpose. This work allows me to follow my own creative rhythms and nurtures my spirit and intellectual interests. I feel united with the rhythm of life at my very core.

I approach my new career with a new sense of confidence and excitement. I know that I can easily manifest a career path which inspires me and gives me a focus and a feeling of purpose. I am able to earn over $500,000 a year yet still maintain a connection to my spiritual life.

In my new job I work from home and enjoy travel to beautiful places and interesting people who are supportive and encourage me to continue to grow and learn. I feel a sense of direction and feel grateful that my success enables me to help others.

I work in a supportive environment that includes a diverse group of dynamic and intelligent people that provide lots of intellectual stimulation and excitement. My office environment is spacious and full of light, providing me with a sense of comfort and ease as well as stability and security.

I am easily able to quickly find a job that will support my financial and emotional needs. I earn at least $_____ every month doing work that I enjoy, and working in an environment of supportive and friendly coworkers.

To open up to more creativity:

My life unfolds with beauty in a creative and dynamic way, full of meaning and texture.

I easily open my heart to the divine creativity that flows within me, and as I work the results of the creative impulse take shape before my very eyes.

To make more time in your life:

I enjoy the time I spend creatively, because it helps me to connect with myself on a deeper level. I feel comfortable taking time off to enjoy my life and I know that there will be plenty of time for me to complete all of my responsibilities.

I accomplish every task set before me with remarkable effectiveness, and there is always plenty of time to do all of the things that I enjoy.

I find it easy to budget and organize my time, knowing that my priority is the time I have with my family.

To find a new home or improve the home you have:

I live in a lovely and comfortable home on the edge of town near the ocean. There are trees and wooded areas and I can see hills and the beauty of nature. My home has lots of windows and light and feels very friendly and familiar to me. The community is welcoming and it is easy to build friendships with like-minded and supportive people.

My home is a reflection of myself that cradles me throughout the day. My home is very warm and luxurious and very comfortable – it truly feels like home. I feel peaceful and happy there, surrounded by beautiful colors and furnishings. My home is easily affordable and an excellent investment in a very convenient location so that I can go anywhere with ease. There are lots of places to walk my dogs through areas that are beautifully landscaped with lots of greenery and flowers. There is a place to garden and grow roses and bougainvilleas.

To improve your health:

I wake up each morning feeling refreshed and full of energy, ready to accomplish all of the tasks set before me. I eat just the right amount of delicious foods that nourish me and get plenty of exercise. I love the way my body feels - young, active, strong and free from pain.

I am in the best of health, feeling vibrant and full of energy.

My surgery is successful and I feel vibrant and alive. The cancer cells in my body shrink and disappear, and my new sense of power fills my entire body with a balanced sense of well-being.

My health continues to improve every day. I feel strong and full of energy and able to balance my work priorities with my personal needs. There is always plenty of time to do everything that I want to do.

I look forward every day to long walks in the woods which energize and inspire me to nurture and care for my body. I enjoy planning and preparing my meals daily, and eat exactly the right amount of delicious foods that nourish and satisfy me. Caring for my physical needs gives me a sense of safety and security and I am able to relax knowing that all of my needs are being met.

To improve your relations with others:

I feel completely accepted by my family and friends for who I am and without conditions. I feel empowered and able to choose those that I welcome into my life.

My relationships with others are balanced and mutually supportive and those around me want to support me and connect with me just as I do them.

I feel connected to a loving community of friends that nurture me and offer help and solace. I feel safe reaching out to friends for help and support and know that I will be cared for no matter what happens.

For more confidence and to feel empowered:

I confidently express my emotions and feelings to those around me, and they in turn respect and admire me for my special gifts.
I am a woman of courage - ready to take on new challenges and lead a more exciting and adventurous life. I feel energized and powerful, knowing that I can overcome any obstacle that is set in my way, and old fears and blocks easily fall away.

I feel happy and content inside, knowing that I have all of the intelligence, personal power and good fortune to be able to succeed at everything in life. I enjoy looking at myself in the mirror, because there are parts of me that are just fabulous! I feel pretty and attractive, and deserving of all good things in life.

I am successful in my personal life and in my professional life, and feel confident in everything I do. I'm comfortable being a powerful woman and easily able to assert myself without intimidating others. I am well-liked by friends and colleagues and the people I work with. I easily move through challenging moments in my life, effortlessly releasing all fears and barriers to transformation and self-realization. I feel myself blossoming into a new sense of my own power and abilities.

For difficult times and psychological work:

I feel comfortable and safe as I begin to explore the buried emotions from my past. I allow my heart to open and I know that as I release the painful experiences I will become healthier and happier. The powerful person that I have become is a valuable ally for the child within that still suffers and I am the one who can release both of us from the past.

I easily and effortlessly release myself from the wounds of the past and feel an incredible sense of joy, freedom and excitement, knowing that I can do anything that I want to do.

To find a supportive community:

I am a welcome member of a group of people who are down to earth, intelligent, interesting and fun to be with. I feel comfortable interacting with them and feel supported by their community. I am confident and know that I have much to offer all of my friends and that they all appreciate me and see my value.

I easily meet friends in my neighborhood that are open-minded and share my interests. I enjoy the support that this social network brings to me.

My life is full of supportive people who nourish my dreams and appreciate me for exactly who I am.

For a more rewarding spiritual life:

I easily connect with my spiritual guidance and higher self, and feel aligned with my purpose. I gladly embrace the path that I am given to the unfolding of my inner life.
I wake up every morning grateful to begin my spiritual practice which nourishes and gives me strength. I am free from any concepts of how this practice should be done and know that whatever time I begin is the perfect time. I feel stabilized, grounded, and completely connected from this practice.

I feel at peace within myself, and easily able to maintain that sense of inner peace no matter what happens in my world.

To free yourself from fear:

I joyfully reinvent myself in every aspect of my life, and each transformation brings me more and more happiness, peace and security.

I live my life free from fear, appreciating every moment of life and good health. The life force within me is strong and powerful, and my vitality increases each and every day.

I allow my life to unfold each day with joy and beauty.
I feel at peace and in balance in my life. I wake up every morning feeling powerful and full of confidence. I know that I have the strength to overcome every challenge that comes my way.

To lose weight:

(weight is a complicated issue and has very little to do with dieting. But when you create an intention to achieve your ideal weight, your psyche will begin to make the psychological and emotional changes that are required for you to be able to release the extra weight. This process can take quite some time so be patient):

I feel healthy and energized and happy with the way my body feels and looks. I weigh ___[specify] pounds and feel great about myself. I eat just the right amount of delicious foods that nourish and satisfy me.

I am easily able to return my metabolism to an active state. Excess weight effortlessly drops off and I feel energized and enjoy the strength of my lean body.

To take better care of yourself:

I enjoy taking all of the time that I need to take care of myself, with long and relaxing walks and baths. The presence of beauty and nature soothes me, and I effortlessly relax deeply into a state of calm and peace.

I am in the greatest shape of my life and feel fantastic, thanks to my daily exercise routine. I sleep well and feel balanced, energized and relaxed. I easily make time for exercise and look forward to it every day.

For better sleep:

I sleep soundly through the night, knowing that I am safe in a cocoon of protection. I am unbothered by noises and movement in the bed, knowing that these do not pose any threat to my safety.

Chapter Thirteen:
Now it's your turn!

Now it's time for you to perfect your language and finalize the powerful vision statements that will begin immediately to transform your life. Take each one of the statements you worked on in the last section and read through it several times. Is there anything in the language that doesn't feel right? Use your internal barometer and if there is anything in the statement that gives you a bit of pause, take a few deep breaths and see what else is needed.

I suggest that you begin your list with this statement which will help set the stage: "I easily and quickly accomplish every one of my goals, and I effortlessly manifest all that I wish for." I've already used it to start your list, which you'll find on the next page.

This is the fun part, so let your creativity flow!

My Vision Statements

I easily and quickly accomplish every one of my goals, and I effortlessly manifest all that I wish for.

Chapter Fourteen: Developing a Practice

Read vision statements at least once a day, and twice is better.

It takes a consistent effort to retrain the subconscious mind. If you create your new vision and write statements to affirm that vision it will be better than nothing, but it will not take long for your subconscious mind to reinstall your old belief systems. This will make it difficult to progress and evolve.

The best time to read your vision statements is first thing in the morning when you wake up, and just before bed. At these times your mind is pliable and ready to take in new information. Reading out loud can be helpful as it uses not only the mind, but also the breath, the voice, the heart and the lungs to create new information.

Visualizing and using as many senses as possible also helps to make the vision more powerful. Hear the sounds of the vacation; feel the upholstery of the furniture or the touch of a lover.
Pay attention to any discomfort in the body.

Your vision statements should be strong and powerful and accurate for you and the new vision that you have created. When you read them, there should be a strong **YES** within your heart, telling you that this is exactly what your soul has been longing for. If any of your statements do not ring loudly with that **YES**, tweak the language so that it aligns more perfectly with your vision.

If when reading your statements you feel some discomfort such as a sudden headache, tightening in the heart, an inability to breathe deeply, or a cramp in the body, this is a signal of a deep blockage (usually fear of some kind) within you that has reacted to the possibility of the change that you are creating.

If this occurs, simply stop reading your list and instead sit quietly, softening around the heart and relaxing your body. Breathe deeply until the feeling subsides. Invite these feelings to send you messages and to instruct you as to their nature. You will likely discover something new from the subconscious mind or the heart that will give you greater guidance.

Once you feel more relaxed and open, continue your practice.

Watch your language!!

Mental messages that undermine our confidence and block us from manifesting our goals and desires are simply habits of thought and language. Try to observe your thought patterns and be aware when your thoughts turn to the negative, or when you find yourself engaging in negativity in your speech.

When you hear yourself saying or thinking something that is less than positive or enthusiastic, stop yourself with a laugh and rewind the tape. Right there and then, reword the negative statement into something positive and powerful; something that will instill you with confidence and certainty.

Use tools to strengthen your focus.

Some people find it useful to create a Vision Board. Using a large bulletin board or a notebook, cut out photos from magazines that depict the feelings or the things that you desire, and keep it where you can see it daily.

The Vision Board will help you to imagine more clearly, but should not be a substitute for the vision statements which penetrate to the level of the subconscious mind to change the core beliefs.

You may find it helpful to set up a small altar somewhere in your home or office which helps to provide a sense of the sacred and assist in your focus as you petition the Universe to facilitate the personal growth and transformation that is taking place.

Meditation is a powerful tool that will help you to quiet the conscious mind and connect more deeply with the higher self that speaks to us from within. As the mind quiets and becomes more calm, the subconscious mind is more accessible and the vibrational patterns stored therein can be more easily altered by the repatterning that this program provides.

Consistency is the key.

I wish that I could say that every one of my Visioncrafting clients was successful, but that is not the case. Creating the vision statements is a powerful beginning, but if we stop there the blocks and negative thinking that reside in our subconscious mind reassert themselves and the desired change does not occur. This then reinforces the belief that change is not possible.

Continuing to read your vision statements regularly will help to create the permanent change that you desire, and will empower your life in many other ways. As we realize more fully the ability that we have to bring about change and expansion with the power of conscious choice, our lives and the lives of everyone around us are forever transformed.

Chapter Fifteen:
Visioncrafting for a Lifetime

I have been working with this practice for almost twenty years. I may go for long periods of time where I leave my Vision list in a drawer, but when my life is not going the way I want it to or I want to make changes, I dust off the list and update it for my current situation. Then I read it twice a day and change comes quickly. My husband Rich says, "Every time you read your goals you really make things happen!" And it's true!

After you've worked with this process for awhile it becomes second nature and transformation comes quickly. You will also become more attuned to your inner guidance and will be aware of the desires that come from ego, and the desires that come from the higher Self. Desires that originate from the higher Self manifest quickly because these desires point us towards our destiny.

If you feel you need some coaching, I am available to assist. An intuitive reading utilizing the tools of astrology can help to facilitate this process and help to devise the most powerful language possible.

I invite you to write me with your experiences, and I encourage you to make Visioncrafting a daily practice and make its magic your own!

Astrodynamics

*Intuitive astrology and Tarot
with Lynn Hayes*

www.astrodynamics.net

866-575-LYNN   lynn@astrodynamics.net

Made in the USA
Lexington, KY
07 May 2014